where the petals grow

ISBN: 979-8-9991270-0-6 (Paperback)

where the petals grow

BY
RAGHDAH G.

part one

FROM THE MARGINS, UNFILTERED

not all is spoken by word,

some meaning is smudged through each page.

notebook lines assigning boundaries,

ink leaking beyond the margins.

through meetings of families,

through espresso and pastry hangouts,

your mother's words are heard far louder than the

rattling of our coffee cups.

empathy flows for your stories,

yet a piercing identification with your mother's.

the women generations ahead,

their harrowing tales—

struggles worn and weathered.

ancestral cycles another ended thirty years ago—

I must have lost track of time and assigned similar dues to myself.

the work,

the cycles to end,

fights sworn to never pass onto another.

the weight tossed into my palms to hold—

to shatter with none other than my two hands.

III

a string of defense

to hide the stain running down the hand that swung the sword.

drew a scene of their own bleeding out,

shed tears over it.

prayed for it—

despite such a wield of pride in another crumbling under their weight.

betrayal marked on the blade,

no pride in that.

we've seen your hands—

the markings you carry to show strength.

the blood staining each epidermal ridge.

i will initiate the conversations to be had.

perhaps i argue at a violent blaze—

words like water.

there is no solitude in walking on eggshells,

nor in softening the cushions behind deliberately spewed injustice.

there is light in walking directly along the line of

each cracked shell another walks around.

injustice should enrage each ear that is shot with the justification of it.

please, find discomfort in my presence—

do not find my ears nor mind to be your safe haven.

faith is not packaged with pride nor arrogance.

is it truly spirituality if it mimics the one banished

from His Mercy on account of that very ego?

citadel of straw, reflective walls.

each exit circles back to the entrance.

mirrors all around,

prose cracking into each pane.

mirrors surround us—

yet the truth hardens.

a building built to reflect

only intends to silence.

made to believe you carved your image into every wall,

that you crafted each brick—

that your outline is embedded into each wall falling around you,

but reality does not stand on scaffolds of illusion.

i cradle anger and resentment and feel for each ridge and

fissure—sharp ends pointing at me as though I sculpted it all;

a reminder of the threat to punch anger and resentment into form.

take their name,

rip the label off,

repackage it as your own—

pride living in lack of growth.

tie their heart strings together as one and name it a favor;

label the world through your myopia,

claim it as final.

your self-imposed obstacles—

gift us the same handcrafted blocks.

demand grateful hands,

listening ears,

and obedient minds.

flick a match, light a fire.

but it'll burn through its own foundation before touching

what truly stands.

cracking under its own weight,

because justice does not fail to trace the footsteps of fallacies.

they will spew that it is *merely* a matter of honor,

yet push for the face of dishonor.

'*a matter of continuing the values of those who preceded us*',

yet push for the morally void to lead us.

the matter is not of honor—

but the preservation of the venom coursing through veins;

dominance intertwining with inheritance.

praise is awarded to what feels like that home.

yet a push for the hollow never fails to be met with a shove into

destruction.

avoid knocking on rooms that require claw marks on its doors to

earn a seat;

to sharpen hands into blades and words into steel.

what's earned by bleeding isn't earned,

it's sacrificed.

voices echo through,

yet the call comes from shaky ground.

labels are found carved into each brick—

hoping you'll trace each curvature,

staining yourself with each label.

walls blackened with soot;

hands stained in writings of each name tarnished.

no blade sharp enough to cut into brick walls, however.

no label heavy enough to crack the truth.

signatures etched onto papers unseen;

blame scorched into promises made in silence.

refusal—sanctioned.

awareness—dismissed.

will—condemned.

but force is not inherited, no.

disagreement is not an offense.

is it that my delivery is callous—

that my tone aims to wound?

should i soften the edges of what burns?

the topic at hand,

was it soft when inflicted?

they ensured they speared through the backs of others but aimed

with love—

does the thought count here?

should i concern myself with the blood staining your blouse

before addressing its host?

sacrifice is the minimum, anything less a question of character.

so sacrifice all of what you are.

but not too much,

for that would read as fragility.

stand strong,

but not too strong—

avoid threatening the boundaries of those you sacrifice for.

for they demand the skin off your back as a prerequisite for respect,

with their own limits towering over you.

applauded for strength,

shamed for the strain.

the skin off the back worn thin under the weight of everyone else.

no scars preferable,

although the lack of durability, not so much.

strength with no growth,

sacrifice with no scars to show for it.

a collar labeled as dignifying,

protection in a punch.

neutrality.

finger is not on the trigger,

no condemnation either.

bystander.

internal fight,

yet no word to utter.

the narcissist knows no bounds;

the soulless utilize all.

the words of God speaking to their oppression—

read merely to be weaponized.

sifting through the highest rules,

the guidelines of the universe

and retaining only what they desire to

misconstrue.

they dig their blades into others,

rip it out, and carry it on their heads as a souvenir;

shame finding no host but the wounded.

each level of power

ensured to be clutched in the palms of their hands.

obligations misconstrued to rob from the vulnerable

to relabel the protected.

not a protector,

nor powerful—a predator starved of strength and honor.

honor is not composed of falsehood,

oppression,

nor the justification of it.

adrenaline pushes you through,

you drag yourself the rest of the way.

push through, **move forward.**

rip the label off,

repackage it all,

for they do not label what they do not carry—

what belongs to you.

the louder their voice,

the deeper it roots.

a healer.

hold your hands out,

let ache spill into your palms;

every tear wiped from your face stained with another's greed.

contamination.

unsatisfied unless you pump their pain through your veins.

words listened to and tossed aside—

yet its echoes scorched the walls

as if it were hammered in louder than it was known.

identity—

tucked close,

held tight,

and snatched in a single motion.

as if it were timber to seize and toss into the blaze.

but energy does not burn.

take what you mistook for the world,

but it will remain unscathed.

care is for your keeping, first.

it's in the words crafted to steady,

not to wind you.

it's not in the doubt drawn to circle you, no. it's *not* in the care that

finds you only to carve your vulnerability into a map.

gentle and quiet— you need not bleed to prove yourself worthy of it.

care is in the calm, not the blade.

strength is applaudable,

conventional,

beautiful.

but how strength is built is overlooked—

side-eyed.

as if looking grit in the eye might conscript them next.

skin trained for war

beneath the armor of a man.

femininity weak;

vulnerability deserving its wounds.

silence is spacious.

i could decorate,

but there's something unsettling about these walls.

they stand tall,

surely they should be creaking with each footstep—

yet they don't falter.

silence is spacious—

far too spacious.

no noise to rival,

only stillness piercing the air—

seemingly threatening stillness.

perhaps when walls have only echoed words seared in fire

and foundations collapse should a footstep dare to stand tall,

stillness is questionable.

only in the calm are the leftover cracks of ember heard.

part two

FOR YOU, FOR ME

stinging ache,

yet no slash in sight.

a doorknob twisted shut,

and its door scratched raw from the clawing on the other side.

hardly any simplicity in locking a room lit by light i laced into its ceilings.

that same glow illuminates the cracks in the wall—

its foundation threatening collapse.

but there is no scarcity,

rebuild.

prioritize self,

with no negotiation.

in the quiet,

admission finds its voice.

a mere whisper,

almost as if apology stitches lesions.

a cackle laced with declaration.

strength resides in faith.

with each time intuition is pushed aside, it grows quieter.

an answered prayer, a wish fulfilled—felt before it is experienced.

yours to have,

yours to trust.

much of the weight you carry as your own,

belongs to the people around you.

it slips from the hands of others,

and is left on your shoulders.

give emotions room to flow without them finding other ways to speak to you.

goalposts shift at the pace of growth,

but progress does not cancel fulfillment.

rage, fury, anger;

sorrow, grief, despair—

not on opposite sides.

each walking the same side, alternating which one stands tall.

sometimes, unnamed.

coated in shame, maybe.

felt, heard, and recognized, nonetheless.

soften their edges,

accept.

allow them to walk through

and out.

i am not a mirror,

i do not reflect back what glares my way—

not the bitterness,

nor the fire.

i do not lift what's thrown at my feet.

your fire burns,

i will not touch it in revenge.

silence is not always surrender.

oftentimes, it's preservation.

preservation of boundaries,

preservation of serenity.

the strongest walls are often built with no witnesses.

i will grab onto my worries

and carve the confidence in His mercy

into each of their ridges.

i'll plead with Him to enhance the illusion that the claw marks are not my

own—

that i did not have to stab through each fissure of doubt myself.

faith has never been promised to wield with ease—

yet remains unconditionally woven into our being.

low voice in the backdrop,

inner conversations—

whispers proven out of alignment with where you walk now.

look further,

the very stem and root—

sprouted from remnants that no longer hold a spot within you.

healing may manifest in resentment;

even in the anger, the questioning, the doubt—

perhaps in the occasional return to what was,

from which you gather yourself once more

and continue moving forward.

all is well,

because healing is not found solely in hope and light.

anger is armor crafted in the moment;

doubt arises in the face of the unfamiliar,

and reversion is not failure.

my nails dig into the palms of my hand,

roses held tight in my fist.

we choose softness in a system that shoves behind us at every step,

counting on our grip to falter—for our roses to roll out of our grasp.

is half the fight protecting delicateness—preserving its authenticity?

a bouquet blossoming in roses.

its petals are held away from the flame,

yet they are not flammable.

each petal tangled around another,

a soft arrangement to please—

yet grasped onto lest the faintest breeze set it ablaze.

but the flame is not yours,

and roses are not flammable.

the ones that belong

read you to understand—

to meet you halfway.

connection does not pair with ingenuity,

and true resonance does not strain easy.

understood when words fall apart,

received without a plot.

fight or flight:

it forges restlessness—

unease when confronted with serenity.

a blessing is not lined with consequence;

love and compassion are all around us, ours to claim.

consider that anxiety is the result of newfound peace that does not

yet know how to settle in.

we are all works in progress;

acknowledge it, and allow it to flow.

growth is not an assignment,

but an endless journey.

stick figures, flowers.

pink ink stains each of my fingertips.

a soft shade of pink, that is.

i sift through a palette of shades to find the perfect pink,

almost like i did decades ago;

digging through a dozen sticks of chalk to grab the same shade of pink

to scratch all over the sidewalk.

disillusionment, flowers.

my voice hoarse from the glass i cough up to spit back at the falsity

being aimed at my face—

yet still sure to find my perfect shade of pink

to illustrate the face of such ferocity.

rage that only sharpens to protect—

although with its ricochet, it doesn't appear so.

stick figures, disillusionment, flowers—

stems with thorns to prick the suffocating grasp.

XLVIII

growth does not require approval,

nor does visibility validate it.

absence of notice does not mean absence of change.

with truth, growth prevails.

ensure your spirituality is intentional —

feeding devotion

rather than depleting it.

the ego, mistaken for truth,

can be unraveled.

so long as you are willing to recognize its presence,

not one trait or habit is fixed in place.

avoid shame in living in alignment with yourself.

reflect on whether a group asking of you to shell out your being

to accept only the remnants of you,

is a group where you belong.

clapping,

cheering,

praise;

apologies held hostage until the curtains part for an audience.

neutrality,

silence;

compassion awaiting the cue of the crowd.

i keep my softness held gently,

with no greed.

mine to grow,

mine to hide—

softness is my inheritance.

defense is on demand,

but dulling the blade follows no clock.

resentment and anger may not be inherently negative emotions—

at least not as a rule.

rather, it's in how they are then wielded that determines whether they

become negative, neutral, or possibly constructive.

resentment is merely a reaction, and anger is paired alongside it—

often intending to protect.

recognize it,

observe it,

and decide which way to move forward.

reconsider what deserves the strength of your grasp.

avoid nurturing what pricks at the palms of your hand;

hold onto what does not steal from what you are.

i tear at the layers of stained glass,

clarity peeking through each pane torn off.

the warm light feels cold to the touch,

yet illuminates smiles that now read crooked.

no correction in mischaracterization,

let it flow.

the wrong label stuck onto the wrong face,

deliberate.

correction reaches no mind that aims to misread.

do not ignore pained parts of you—

once you allow your emotions to speak their side,

affirm.

affirm that living in a position of lack leaves little

room for what you desire,

nor what you envision to be.

what holds blessings

may not have room to hold self deprecation.

glass shattered,

scattered over the floor.

unsure what pieces belong,

what to pick up.

the fear of shards cutting into fingers leaves them left unclaimed.

ignore.

forfeit ownership.

another will walk through mindlessly.

shards will prick into their soles.

another will pick it all up.

and unbeknownst to the one to gather it,

such duty was not theirs to bear.

my fingers tug around a thread braided into dozens more.

pulled taut,

yet the integrity of each to weave beyond it, intact.

intertwined upon each inch of thread—

yet only discolored ends cut loose.

sharpness and softness are two ends of the same spectrum—

existing simultaneously, on the same path.

one needs not be shoved aside in order for the other to thrive.

rather, they take root in different corners of the same field.

surrounded by a garden of thorns, wield the sharp truth.

surrounded by what waits to bloom, let love pour into it.

there is light in responsibility.

responsibility in connections,

words,

and consideration.

where the focus shifts to obligation,

sincerity is lost.

what does not honor depth is not owed response.

no desire to water what has wilted.

nor to reach for sharp stems

believing thorns are taught softness.

new growth is in allowing space to bloom.

stems and roses;

thorns and petals.

i tie each stem to every rose,

bound together by devotion,

trusting they stand on their own.

soft aroma of the flora;

thorns poking out of each stem do not prick at my palms,

mine to hold.

the past prayers I actively experience,

the prayers I once pleaded for,

now a part of my mundane day-to-day.

in stillness,

and in motion,

let the gentle presence of the ordinary

intertwine with gratitude.

let boundaries exist in silence,

without announcement—

without permission.

forgiveness to abandon the ache,

remembrance to shield.

no dagger is carried forward,

but its entry wound scars—

the scar burning when a gesture mirrors what drove it in.

etched to remind, should hollow apologies speak.

gratitude in His mercy,

to be given permission to ask the Lord for my desires.

to plead to The Almighty, who creates every next second and minute.

trembling hands and aching chests.

scrambling to warmth with a match in hand

and disillusionment clouding entryways.

shadows etched across the walls,

each shaped to a memory.

ache inflated to weakness—

yet it stands as the lit candle in an empty room should one revisit.

whether to snuff the flame,

or to relight the space

with softer aromas to coat walls that don't weep.

a glow that does not burn,

only warms.

release—

not to abandon,

but to reflect the faith drawn into my essence.

the trust treading alongside doubt,

spilled together across the gentle hold of the prayer mat.

a branch stretches past the edge of your view

just enough to know it roots deep—

flourishing where your eyes don't follow.

the most blooming flora grow with or without spotlight.

fruit growing for your harvest,

not yet within reach.

not all goodness needs a view,

choose to believe anyway.

vulnerability exiled;

a round of applause runs for armor,

yet flinches at softness.

shrinking into a shell in the name of wisdom,

authenticity branded as idiocracy.

to have truly grown is to be true to self,

to give and receive genuinely.

hesitation in the face of apology is not a cruelty—

nor should it be rushed.

forgive and forget,

but sometimes forgetting is in release—

a space not quite a grudge,

and not yet forgiveness.

gathering dust, not weight.

peripheral vision.

i see loose ends forcefully pulled through the fabric of reality.

a squint to glare at the calloused hands to do so—

the fingers to point in blame of the yarn scattered over the floor,

while the other hand continues tearing apart knots and weaves.

knots that were gently tied together,

my trust—

it was interwoven.

woven through and out.

trust; knots.

mine to gather,

mine to sew back together.

you're allowed to hold pain in one hand

and a plan in the other.

the ache does not nullify movement.

defense is not disgrace;

avoid mistaking strength for silence in the courtroom

where your pain stands trial.

up for denial,

up to wipe from your memory if you allow it so.

their own weight held in the palms of their hands

and yet they stumble over the load of it.

sculpted and shaped to their liking—

still they flinch at the sight of it.

letting go of conflict as a weapon of choice is a strength.

isolating from what threatens

to maintain long-built serenity—

to lay down the shield before war is declared over.

first generation.

but love did not start with me—

warm meals and henna plastered fingertips did not start with me.

the softest fire,

lit by hands more delicate than my own.

words inherited with fear laced between syllables,

spoken by mouths that grit even under vice.

hands made to feed,

never to write.

i'll tug at the thread—

gently.

loosen each stitch with the tips of my fingers;

sew sentences back together with prose.

my hands shaped to feed,

to write,

to softly crochet my mother's threads into new patterns.

fabric not solely to warm—

but to decorate.

LXXX

light seeps through the cracked windowpane,

illuminating without demand—

as though the rugged glass it enters through can soften in its stillness.

wound mending starts at the deepest level and onward,

scarring does not invalidate healing,

nor does it indicate a lack of growth.

a crack of sunlight may illuminate over it,

and no question will follow.

to allow warmth into orbit is to solidify self-regard.

to accept any less than faithfulness calls the self into question—

puts world view on display,

and reveals the voice in the mirror.

vulnerability did not forge this softness,

she has always been here.

tucked away at times;

out of sight,

always in mind.

hidden never meant abandonment,

only that strategy and chess are refused.

what is delicate is surrounded by authenticity.

explanation loses weight when clarity is found in isolation.

fragments glued together to make sense of it—

to listen for echoes of clarification.

peace does not make a lightning appearance.

it's in the words that now roll off the tongue without a punch,

the voice spoken with softened corners,

and the traits once tucked away

no longer seeking permission to be visible.

the rawest forms of hope have required utmost discipline to nurture.

to dig through glass to pluck out remnants of faith

that had been waiting to rebuild upon another vase.

the wonder infused with it all— never weakness.

a house miles away,

familiarity stinging the air of its front yard.

the lights inside are always on,

spilling warmth across the sidewalk.

i'm welcome to visit, apparently.

yet all i do is stare idly when my path crosses it.

i'd know my way around—each hallway and every turn.

yet i'll pluck only a rose from the garden outside and move forward.

i know this place, apparently.

i lit the lights inside and left it behind.

thin walls,

and it appears warm—only when winter falls outside.

breezy and brittle on the inside,

and the doorknob pricks—

but not for me.

ink bleeds through the softest of pages,

to protest on behalf of fury,

i'd have thought such volatile chemistry would set the pages ablaze,

yet they combine to speak ever so delicately.

bouquet of roses:

a hundred could bloom,

yet the scent lingers with just twelve.

fragrance trailing beyond its garden;

petals tracing the signature of its flower.

evolve without abandoning your essence,

give love while keeping yours.

About the Author

Raghdah G. is a multidisciplinary Arab-American writer whose work examines the intersections of emotional nuance and resilience.

Outside of writing, Raghdah is pursing a degree in educational studies. *Where the Petals Grow* is her debut poetry collection, and she continues to develop her work across multiple genres.